RUGBY
SKILLS

RUGBY SKILLS

Will Carling

with
Ian Robertson

Queen Anne Press

A QUEEN ANNE PRESS BOOK

First published in 1994 by
QUEEN ANNE PRESS
a division of
Lennard Associates Limited
Mackerye End
Harpenden
Herts AL5 5DR

A catalogue entry is available from the British Library

ISBN 1 85291 555 2

Edited by Caroline North
Photographs by Colorsport
Reproduction by Leaside Graphics
Cover design by Cooper Wilson

Printed and bound in Spain

CONTENTS

FOREWORD

Without dreams, youth is hardly worth having. It is the golden time when every fantasy is still a possibility, when every ambitious thought has yet to battle against hard reality.

It is time, too, when heroes are uncomplicated – you see them with a clear-eyed acceptance of their talent and ability. They are heroes because they are brilliant at what they do.

Ideally, all youngsters should have the chance to chase their ambitions. This book, I hope, will help the current generation who aspire to run out at Twickenham, Lansdowne Road, Cardiff or Murrayfield. Ambition, after all, needs to be linked to knowledge and skill if it is to be fulfilled.

Some of rugby's current heroes show in this book the skills and techniques that they have acquired. They demonstrate that the basic arts of rugby are neither complicated nor hard to understand.

They cannot demonstrate, however, the crucial part that constant practice has to play. I grew up in the age of the gifted amateur, but, believe me, they became more and more gifted the harder they practised.

If this book helps someone achieve their ambitions, or just increase their enjoyment of playing the game, Heinz will be well satisfied. I believe that rugby is a sport that offers special rewards to those who play it. It is no game for the weak-hearted nor those who are mean of spirit. Played and enjoyed in the right manner, it can give a set of rules for living that enriches all our lives.

Tony O'Reilly

INTRODUCTION

I have been very fortunate in the last few years to have played in a very successful England side which reached the final of the 1991 World Cup and which won Grand Slams in 1991 and 1992. One common factor which is shared by all top players is a mastery of the basic skills of the game. Every player, forwards and backs alike, should be able to pass, catch, tackle and kick.

Any comparison of a dozen great international stars will show that each player has his own individual style and a slightly different emphasis will be placed on certain facets of the game in New Zealand, Australia, South Africa and the four Home Unions. But all the top players rely on a sound and thorough grounding in the basic skills. Once a good technique has been achieved each individual will be able to derive the maximum satisfaction and enjoyment from playing rugby.

There is a natural inclination for most players to spend a lot of time practising what they are already quite good at and they often tend to ignore the aspects of the game which they do not do quite so well or do not particularly enjoy doing. Too often players concentrate on perfecting kicking with their right foot at the expense of learning to kick at all with their left foot. It is important for every player to be at least competent at kicking with either foot Similarly, most players prefer to do most of their tackling favouring one shoulder but everyone should be able to tackle equally well with either shoulder– as the technique is exactly the same, it is simply a question of practice.

Every skill demands a great deal of practice but the rewards are well worth it because, just like riding a bicycle, once the skill has been learned it will never be forgotten.

The game has changed and developed quite significantly in the course of my ten years in senior rugby, but one fact has remained constant: a practical knowledge of all the fundamental skills is just as important as ever.

With the help of over 200 photographs I have tried to show in this book that rugby is a relatively simple, straightforward game. I think every skill is clearly and concisely explained and illustrated.

Each skill demands hours of dedicated practice. There are no short cuts. Nevertheless, the effort pays real dividends in the long term. Admittedly, not

every player who reads this book and practises the various disciplines will go on to play international rugby, but he will maximise his own potential and that is what everyone should aim at trying to achieve.

Above all, training, practising and playing should be equally enjoyable, but it still goes without saying that the higher the standard you reach, the greater the satisfaction and fun you will derive from playing rugby.

The better every individual is, the better the team will be and at this stage of my career I am really glad that I put in the effort when I was young to try to master the game's basic skills.

Will Carling
August 1994

ACKNOWLEDGEMENTS

I would like to begin by expressing my grateful thanks to the two sponsors of the book, Heinz and Next. I am delighted that they have supported this project and helped to make it such a glossy production. I really appreciate the encouragement I have received from Tony O'Reilly, president of H.J. Heinz, and David Jones, chief executive of Next.

Two of the players in the England squad deserve special mention for their contribution to the finished product. Rob Andrew, the most capped fly-half in world rugby, kindly agreed to demonstrate his skills for the illustrations in the whole chapter on the art of kicking and Kyran Bracken has done the same with the chapter on scrum-half play.

I would also like to thank Rory and Tony Underwood, along with Paul Hull, for all their help in various parts of this book. We were all very fortunate to be given permission by the Natal Rugby Union to use the magnificent King's Park Test ground in Durban for shooting the bulk of the photos which have been used in the book.

I am particularly grateful to Stuart Macfarlane and Colin Elsey of Colorsport for taking so many outstanding photographs.

Congratulations to Clare Robertson for beating the deadline for typing the final script and to Duncan Robertson for impersonating a line-out forward in partnership with Kyran Bracken.

A big thank you, too, to Ian Robertson, coach of Cambridge University from 1971 to 1986, for all his help in the preparation of this book and to Les Cusworth, assistant coach to England, for his practical help at King's Park in Durban.

Adrian Stephenson deserves a special mention for developing and publishing the book. He was ultimately responsible for the finished product.

Just as it should be in rugby, it was a great team effort.

PASSING AND HANDLING

Get the basics right

NEXT

Rugby is a game which is based on the skill of passing and no matter what position the individual plays everyone has to be able to give and take a pass. The whole idea of the game is running, passing, making breaks and scoring tries. Although it may look pretty simple and straightforward, it requires a good technique and plenty of practice. A combination of different skills – balance, timing and accuracy – all need to be in operation at once. It is very important for every player to be able to pass equally well to the right and to the left.

PASSING TECHNIQUE

For mini-rugby players learning to pass, it is best to build up confidence and a sound technique in easy stages. First of all, beginners should get used to simply handling a ball.

Just to familiarise yourself with the ball it is a useful exercise to move it round your body. Always use a ball the correct size for your own age group because if you use one which is too big it makes it far more difficult.

Move it slowly in a clockwise direction behind your back and then continue round to where you started. Do this a dozen times clockwise and then a dozen times anti-clockwise. Speed it up gradually until you are doing it quickly without dropping the ball.

This exercise gives you a good feel for a rugby ball.

Another fun exercise is to have a group of three players passing the ball in a circle, first in a clockwise and then in an anti-clockwise direction and, finally, at random, in any direction.

1. I pass it to Tony Underwood.

2. Tony passes it to his left to his brother Rory.

3. Rory passes it to me.

This exercise demands total concentration and once the players are confident and everyone is passing and catching really well the number of participants can be increased to four, five or six and the circle widened.

1

2

3

Another exercise at the very early stage which instils confidence is:

1. Stand close together, just touching hands, and pass standing still.

2. Rory Underwood hands the ball to me.

3. I rotate on the spot to prepare to hand the ball on.

4. I sweep the ball round towards Tony Underwood.

5. He takes the ball from me.

1

2

3

4

5

For the next step, Rory and Tony move a couple of feet further away from me. Now we make a proper pass.

1

2

3

4

5

1. Rory turns his shoulders and head towards me and his eyes focus on my outstretched hands, which are ready to receive the ball. My hands are Rory's target area. I hold them out towards him with my fingers extended ready to catch the ball.

2. I concentrate on the ball, facing the passer.

3. Having caught the ball, I now turn my head towards *my* target area – the outstretched hands of Tony Underwood.

4. Turning my shoulders, I pass at my target area.

5. Tony takes the ball in his outstretched hands.

Each player should have a turn in the middle.

PASSING ON THE MOVE

Once players have learned to pass well, both to their right and left standing still, it is time to practise passing on the move.

Basic technique

1. Here I have caught the pass to me early, which means that in one sweeping movement I am ready to pass the ball on to the next player.

2. I turn my head to find my target area.

3. My eyes are focused on my target area as I release the ball. My shoulders have turned round slightly towards the receiver and my hands follow through towards him.

1

2

3

Putting it into practice

1. My eyes are firmly focused on the target area – the outstretched hands of the receiver (Rory Underwood). My peripheral vision improves as my head and upper body rotate.

2. My hands follow through, guiding the ball just above waist-height in front of the receiver so that he can run on to it. The ball should always be passed in front of the receiver. Note that Rory watches the ball the whole time, never taking his eyes off it.

3. He takes the ball in both hands without breaking stride.

1

2

3

Exactly the same as the previous sequence,
except that the pass is to my right.

To demonstrate the speed and accuracy of the manoeuvre, which are the most important ingredients of a good pass, it is good to work in groups of three and here I am flanked by Rory and Tony.

It is essential for the receiver always to offer the target area of his hands. As we have seen, the passer must always pass in front of the receiver. It is important that the pace of the pass makes it as easy as possible for the receiver to catch and transfer the ball in one movement. The passer has to be sympathetic to the receiver. In other words, there is no sense in firing a very fast, hard, flat pass to someone on a wet day with a heavy ball.

1. Tony passes at my hands (his target area). I focus on the ball.

2. As soon as I have caught it safely, I begin to rotate my head, eyes and upper body towards Rory.

3. I concentrate on his hands as I sweep the ball across my body and pass in front of him.

4. I follow through with my hands still pointing at the target area.

2

3

4

Exactly the same as the previous sequence, except that this time the pass is to the right.

CATCHING

Every player ought to be able to catch a kick from the opposition, whether he is a full-back or a prop.

The first rule is to keep your eyes on the ball the whole time it is in the air. Once you have found the right spot to make your catch you should brace yourself by standing with your legs about shoulder-width apart.

1. I am under the ball, legs apart for a solid base, with hands ready.

2. As the ball is about to reach me I cradle my arms, with my hands and fingers pointing towards the ball.

3. With my eyes still on the ball, I prepare to make the catch.

4. As I take the ball, I bend my knees to form a solid base.

1

2

3

4

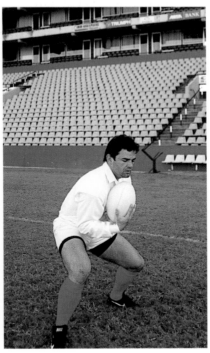

To practise this skill, two players can kick to each other. As confidence grows, you should create a match situation with an extra player.

1. I prepare to take a ball in defence with my nearest team-mate, Rory Underwood, in close support.

2. As I make the catch, Rory is already advancing to help our side secure possession.

3. He begins to bind on me, to come between me and the opposition.

4. Together we have control of the ball to ensure our team keeps possession.

1

2

3

4

With the recent change in the laws, there is now an advantage in jumping up for the ball because the opposition is not allowed to tackle a player with both feet off the ground.

1. Eyes on the ball, waiting for the exact moment to jump up.

2. I take the ball while I am in mid-air so that I cannot be tackled.

3. I land in the braced position, knees bent, ready to absorb the first tackle.

1

2

3

THE ROLLING BALL

Another important handling skill is to be able to gather a bouncing ball in the loose.

1. I approach the ball with my eyes focused on it, preparing to get my body into a squat position.

2. As I collect the ball my feet are almost astride it – the ball is roughly in the middle of my legs. I bend right down from my hips so that I am comfortably balanced as I place both hands on it. My body angle is important. If I don't bend right down with a low centre of gravity I will find it much harder to collect the ball cleanly.

3. I drive off with my right leg and accelerate away.

1

2

3

RUNNING IN ATTACK

Release the man

THE OVERLAP

One of the best sights in rugby is watching a great try being scored either as the result of a brilliant individual piece of skill or after the combined efforts of the whole back division. The easiest way to outmanoeuvre the opposition is simply to create an overlap, or even a half-overlap, in the threequarter line to give the extra bit of space for the player on the wing.

This can be achieved by bringing a running full-back into the line to make the extra man or by using the blind-side wing as an extra player in midfield. A side-step, a swerve, a scissors or a dummy scissors are all ways of creating a half-overlap, and then it often becomes a case of two players being set free with only one defender to beat.

In those circumstances it is essential that the two-against-one situation or the three-against-two situation is turned into a try but all too regularly a player fails to draw the last defender properly, passes too early or runs at the wrong angle and the chance is squandered. The basic skill should be practised first in the two-against-one situation. The ball-carrier must run at the correct angle, which in a normal threequarter movement would be more or less parallel to the touchline. There's no point in running back into the forwards, and far too many back movements nowadays are dead before they start because the backs drift aimlessly across the field at a diagonal angle towards the touchline.

It is very easy for the cover to defend against teams which do this. The key to success is hard, straight running by the whole back division, including the running full-back. As a general rule all the backs in attack should be running near enough parallel to the touchline.

In a two-against-one overlap the first priority is for the player in possession to totally commit the sole defender on to himself and then to time his pass at precisely the right moment to release the extra man. This exercise should be practised in a reasonably confined space, perhaps between the five-metre line and the touchline. Once players have mastered the art of drawing a man in a two-against-one situation, they can advance to three against two, then four against three and even five against four.

If every player runs at the correct angle, straight and hard, draws his opposite number on to him and times his pass to perfection then every time five players face four defenders they should score.

Two against one

1. I am confronted by just one defender, Paul Hull, and I have Tony Underwood with me on the attack.

2. It is my job to commit the defender totally to tackling me. The coaching phrase is to *fix* my opponent. To fix Paul Hull I run straight, even cutting back slightly, away from my wing. I run at the defender's inside shoulder to draw him away from Tony Underwood.

3. By running at the defender's inside shoulder I have created more time and space for the player outside me. I have guaranteed that my opponent is committed to me and he is not able to drift across towards Tony Underwood.

4. I have drawn the defender on to me and by timing my pass properly I have released Tony Underwood so that he can exploit our overlap.

It should be clear that if I had run towards Tony then Paul could have drifted across the field with me, so that when I passed to Tony he could have accelerated on to tackle him and the overlap would have been wasted.

I

2

3

4

This demonstrates exactly the same exercise with the pass this time to my right.

Three against two

Once every player, including prop forwards and locks, is confident of always turning two against one into a score, you can progress to three attackers against two defenders. Precisely the same skills apply. Each attacker runs at the inside shoulder of his opponent and, once he has *fixed* his opponent, passes the ball. The angle of running is crucial and to capitalise on the overlap the timing of the pass is vital. It should also be stressed that the attacking players must maintain the depth of the line. If one player comes up too quickly or too flat, the advantage is lost.

1. Rory Underwood is on the attack and he fixes the first defender in the green shirt, Rob Andrew, by running hard and straight at his inside shoulder. The defender is totally committed.

2. Similarly, I change my angle of running fractionally from a straight line to slightly back towards the source of the possession by aiming at my opponent's inside shoulder.

3. I have committed the defender, Paul Hull, and released the player on the overlap, Tony Underwood. Note here that Rory Underwood, having passed, has run on into Rob Andrew's inside shoulder.

4. Similarly, I have run on into Paul Hull's inside shoulder, which shows I had totally committed him to tackling me. As a result, we have made full use of our three-against-two overlap and Tony Underwood is free on the outside.

At more advanced levels, there can be definite advantages in the centres taking the ball a little flatter and slightly wider. However, it should be noted that the flatter the threequarters align, the better the quality of possession they need, the slicker their handling needs to be, and the more important it is to run at the right angles and to hold the depth of the back line. Speed is of the essence, and all the basics have to be done quickly and accurately as the flatter the alignment is, the narrower the margin of error. The Australian midfield of Lynagh, Horan and Little are experts in using a flat threequarter line to best advantage, and it is something more and more sides are trying to emulate. However, it does require great technique and countless hours of practice.

1

2

3

4

SELLING A DUMMY

It is all very well to describe how to draw an opponent to take full advantage of an overlap, but it is always possible that the defender will not totally commit himself to the player with the ball. If this happens, it is the ideal time to sell a dummy. If you sense that your opponent is more interested in the player in support than in you, the last thing you want to do is pass to your team-mate and then watch him being tackled as he receives the ball.

1. I set off intending to draw the defender and release Tony Underwood.

2. I have angled my run at the defender's inside shoulder but just a split-second before I pass I realise he is not committed to tackling me but is drifting off towards Tony Underwood.

3. Instead of passing, I hold on to the ball and, cutting back inside the defender, I accelerate away.

4. The defender has bought the dummy and has committed himself to tackling Tony. I am through the gap and Tony will be with me in support.

I

2

3

4

THE SCISSORS

A sharp change of direction is a good way to wrong-foot the opposition and it is quite difficult to organise a defence to cope with such a manoeuvre. This is the aim of the scissors between two players and it has the added advantage that if the opposition do not react to the move, it is just as easy to execute a dummy scissors instead. It is up to the ball-carrier to decide on the spur of the moment whether to go through with the scissors or not. He can sense the reaction of the opposition and he should be in control of the situation.

1

2

3

4

1. Instead of running straight and hard, I switch to running diagonally across the pitch, drawing the man marking me in the same direction.

2. As I start my angled run, Rory Underwood alters his direction by cutting back inside me towards the original source of possession.

3. Just before we pass by each other, I turn side-on to the opposition, shielding the ball in the process, and lob it gently in his path. His eyes are focused firmly on the ball.

4. He takes the ball and accelerates away, changing the whole direction of the attack.

THE DUMMY SCISSORS

The dummy scissors can be just as effective as the scissors. It is important that the ball is hidden from the opposition as the player in possession throws the dummy, as this will cause a moment of hesitation in the opposing defence. It will give the ball-carrier the chance to catch the opposition flat-footed and an overlap, or at least a half-overlap, should have been created.

1. I change my angle of running to switch the direction of the attack.

2. As I am about to execute the scissors by passing to Rory Underwood, I sense that the defender, Paul Hull, is more committed to tackling Rory than he is to tackling me.

3. I go through all the motions of carrying out the scissors, but at the very last moment, with the ball hidden from the opposition, I keep possession and at the same time accelerate away.

4. My manoeuvre has caused a hesitation in the opposition defence and I have taken full advantage of it.

I

2

3

4

1

2

THE SIDE-STEP

Arguably the simplest and most dramatic way to change direction is the side-step. To be effective it has to be done at speed and the player should accelerate into it.

The aim is to wrong-foot the opposition by leaning and moving one way before exploding off in the opposite direction. It has to be done in reasonable proximity to the defence, because if you move too early your opponent can change direction with you and if it is done too late he will already be tackling you.

You can practise side-stepping initially by running at a goalpost to get the feel of the movement and then against a player kneeling on the ground. In this sequence I have used a yellow cone as my marker.

3   **4**

1. From running straight at the yellow cone I move to my right about a couple of feet to draw my opponent towards me and catch him slightly off-balance as he leans to his left.

2. I now drive very strongly off my right foot, switching direction quite dramatically.

3. The side-step has covered over three feet in distance and has been done at real speed. Having changed direction sharply, I accelerate away.

4. I now have the choice of straightening the line, having created a gap, or I can continue on my new angle of attack and look for support.

THE SWERVE

Another way of changing direction is the swerve, but it has to be said that this is not a simple ploy for most players. To do it well you have to be a well-balanced runner with genuine acceleration, and if you have these talents a swerve can be devastatingly effective.

1. Rory Underwood approaches the defender, Paul Hull, in a straight line.

2. When he is about four yards away, he suddenly changes direction almost at right-angles. He leans to his left and begins to accelerate with his right leg crossing virtually in front of his left leg.

3. This completely new angle of running, created in a split-second, gives the initiative to the attacker.

4. Having caused a moment of hesitation in the mind of the defenders, Rory uses his explosive speed to accelerate clear.

1

2

3

4

THE HAND-OFF

In any attempt to make a break and beat an opponent there is always a possibility that the defender will still be within range. The hand-off can make the difference between breaking through or being stopped.

1. As the defender approaches, I aim my right hand at his right shoulder whilst tucking the ball under my left arm.

2. As the defender prepares to launch himself into the tackle, I push my right hand firmly into his shoulder whilst at the same time I try to drive away from him.

3. I push his shoulder down and away behind me, ensuring that he is unable to make an effective tackle.

1

2

3

KICKING

Just for kicks

Although rugby is essentially a running, open game there are occasions in every match when it is necessary to kick and it is important that every player is competent at punting the ball. Most of the kicking will be done by the backs but every forward ought to be capable of kicking the ball a reasonable distance with some degree of accuracy, at least with his stronger foot.

All backs should practise kicking with both feet as the technique is exactly the same with either foot. If youngsters make a determined effort to use both feet from a very early age they should soon reach a good standard. Needless to say, good kicking is all about good technique and it is well worth learning and practising the correct technique from the start.

It is amazing how much poor kicking there is in every match – even at international level – and more often than not it is simply a case of weak technique.

Kicking can be used in a variety of different ways, although the technique is similar in all cases. In defensive situations, kicking is used to clear your lines, relieve the pressure and gain enough ground to be ready to relaunch offensives. In attacking situations, the ball is kept in play to put the opposition under the maximum pressure and good, accurate kicking will give a team the best possible chance of regaining possession.

Kicking just for the sake of it with no real motive is the most frustrating aspect of modern rugby. Such kicking merely presents the ball to the opposition. The art of drop-kicking and place-kicking is a more selective and specialised skill and it can make the difference between winning and losing matches at every level.

It is not just the fly-half who might drop the winning goal. A famous Scottish back-row forward, Peter Kininmonth, once dropped a goal from 45 yards at Murrayfield to help Scotland beat Wales. That was the only drop-goal of his whole career! So it is a skill worth having.

There is no substitute for a sound technique and the demonstration of all forms of kicking by Rob Andrew, England's most-capped fly-half and the world record holder for dropped goals in international rugby, should point everyone in the right direction.

PUNTING

One of the key points about kicking is to try to ensure that the ball is at the correct angle as you strike it.

1. This picture shows what you should be aiming to achieve. The ball meets the top of the instep of the foot at exactly the same angle as it leaves your hands, almost flat, but slightly raised at the near end as in pictures 4 and 5.

2. The ball is held at a slight angle with the right hand at the near end and underneath and the left hand at the far end at the side.

3. To maintain the angle of the ball it should not be thrown up in the air but simply dropped straight down.

4. The weight is transferred on to the left foot now, with your head over the ball and your eyes fixed on it.

5. The right foot is free to swing smoothly through and the foot is pointed.

6. At the point of impact the ball is at the same angle at which it was released in picture 3 and the foot remains pointed for maximum effect.

7. You finish with a good high follow-through. The right foot is still pointed, the right leg straight and never bent, with the body leaning back slightly.

The best results are achieved through a smooth action and good timing – not by brute strength.

2

3

4

5

6

7

This sequence shows exactly the same technique
for kicking with the left foot.

THE HIGH, HANGING KICK

There is one interesting kick which players can practise once they have mastered the basic art of punting. Occasionally the fly-half may want to launch a high, hanging kick over the opposition threequarter line somewhere short of the full-back and not too close to the wing. To get the height and make it difficult to catch, the ball is kicked not when it is almost flat, as in a normal punt, but virtually on its end.

1. The ball is held almost vertical with one hand on each side.

2. Just as in a normal punt, the ball is held and released at exactly the angle at which you want it to strike your foot. For a normal kick it is almost horizontal; for this kick it is almost vertical.

3. The weight is on the left leg with the ball about to land on its end on the top of the boot.

4. The right leg straightens on impact and the ball soars skywards, rotating end over end, which makes it quite difficult to judge in flight and tricky to catch.

5. This particular kick demands a high follow-through.

This technique is for this one specialist tactical kick only and should not be used for line-kicking.

I

2

3

4

5

I   2

THE GRUBBER KICK

In a similar vein, there is one other tactical kick which any player might find useful and that is the grubber kick. Rather like the high, hanging kick, the idea is for the ball to be propelled end over end, but this time along the ground and not through the air. It is a very helpful kick for any player who finds himself with the ball outside his own 22-metre line without support. If he kicks directly into touch the line-out will be taken from where he kicked, but if he uses a grubber kick, the line-out will be at the point where the ball goes into touch.

From a good, controlled grubber kick, the ball will bounce along in a pretty straight line. Not only can it be employed to clear to touch, it can also be used in attack to split a defence and allow you and your supporting team-mates to

3   **4**

chase in pursuit. Fly-halves and centres can find it a very useful variation in attack to make opposing threequarter lines think twice before sprinting up in defence.

1. The ball is held with one hand on each side in an almost vertical position. The head is over the ball with the body weight leaning forward.

2. The ball is released to land in a vertical position.

3. Just as the ball lands, it should be simultaneously propelled forward, firmly along the ground. The right knee is bent and nearly level with the ball.

4. The foot is pointed as it is normally for a kick but this time the follow-through is low, driving the ball along the ground.

THE DROP KICK

Of all the ways of scoring points in rugby, the drop kick remains one of the easiest.

1. The ball is held with hands down each side and your body should be at an angle to the posts.

2. The ball is released to drop straight down so that it remains vertical. Your head stays down and your eyes are on the ball.

3. The weight is on the left leg, which is beside the ball as it lands. The right leg is free to swing smoothly through in an arc. The very moment after the ball makes contact with the ground, the right instep swings through and lifts the ball into the air.

4. With the weight still on the left leg, the right leg follows through across the body.

1

2

3

4

THE PLACE KICK

Perhaps the most important attributes to develop are a good consistent rhythm and a sound technique. Quite often when a goal-kicker is out of form, the reason is that he has lost his rhythm or because he is not following the golden rules of planting his non-goal-kicking foot beside the ball, keeping his head over the ball and keeping his head down on the follow-through.

1. The ball should be placed virtually vertically on the tee with one seam facing the kicker. The kicker then lines up the ball with the posts. Here Rob Andrew points to the spot almost one third of the way up the ball where you should strike it.

2. The kicker takes about six or eight paces back at an angle of about 45 degrees to the left of the line through the ball to the goalposts. The angle of the run-up becomes greater the wider the kick is from the posts, so it is nearer to 90 degrees than 45 degrees if the ball is on the left-hand touchline for the right-footed round-the-corner kicker.

I   **2**   **3**

3. The kicker should approach the ball at a steady pace. It is very important to place the left foot just a few inches to the left of the ball and fractionally behind it. At this stage all your weight is on the left leg. The head is down and eyes are fixed on the ball. If the left foot lands too near or too far away from the ball it will spoil the kick. It should land about six inches from the ball to allow the right leg to swing through and across it in a relaxed and rhythmic way.

4. Here Rob is concentrating on striking the ball on the exact spot he pointed out in picture 1.

5. He makes contact with his right instep, keeping his head over the ball and weight on his left leg.

6. The right leg follows through slightly across and in front of the body.

To be a good goal-kicker takes an enormous amount of practice and it demands a great deal of concentration and a solid technique. You must develop balance, timing, rhythm and consistency.

4   **5**   **6**

1   2

SCRUM-HALF KICKING

From the base of a scrum or ruck.

The key factors here are for the scrum-half to give himself time and room to execute the kick in the full knowledge that the opposition will be desperate to tackle him before he kicks or will try to charge down the kick. To make that space, it is often necessary, unless your pack is motoring forward, to take one quick pace towards your own goal-line before hooking the ball over your own forwards and into enemy territory. Speed and agility are the vital combination.

1. The split-second the ball emerges from the scrum or ruck, Kyran Bracken has his hands on it.

2. He quickly pulls it across his body and makes sure he has room to kick almost at the same moment as he scoops up the ball.

3   4   5

3. He releases the ball, keeping his whole body side-on to the opposition, and, taking a short backswing, prepares to hoist the ball over both sets of forwards.

4. Note that the ball lands on the foot at the same sort of angle as when Rob Andrew was punting earlier in the chapter (see pictures 1 and 6 on pages 70 and 71).

5. A good, strong follow-through ensures that the ball will have the elevation to clear the forwards.

Before the scrum goes down, the scrum-half should check his target area for the kick so that he doesn't need to waste any time once the ball surfaces. It is important that he has that mental picture in his mind before he puts the ball into the scrum.

From a line-out

The kick from a line-out is very similar but has the advantage that the scrum-half can already be standing a good yard away from his own forwards. On the other hand, he is very dependent on top-quality possession as he knows he will have very little time to get in his kick. Any palmed possession must be deadly accurate. A catch and drive by the forwards is a little easier.

1. Kyran Bracken stands about four feet from the line-out and as the ball is palmed he gets his hands and feet in the right positions in preparation for an instantaneous kick.

2. In the very act of catching the ball, Kyran is ready to put in his kick.

3. He takes one quick step away from the line-out with his body side-on to the forwards.

4. At the same time, he releases the ball, trying to ensure that it lands at the correct angle and almost horizontal on to his boot.

5. With a short backswing he hoists it over his forwards down the line of touch to gain valuable ground.

6. With the short backswing, the follow-through is not quite as high as in a normal punt, but it is still done with a straight leg and pointed foot and plenty of power.

1

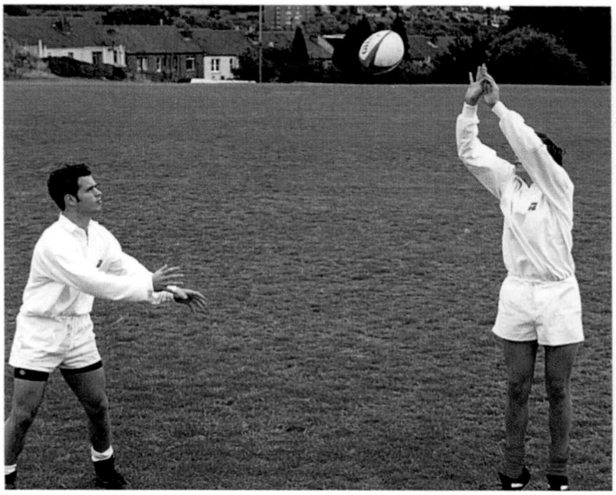

2

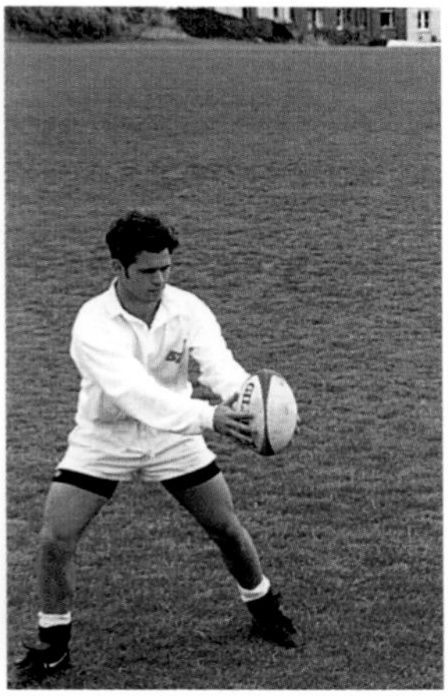

3

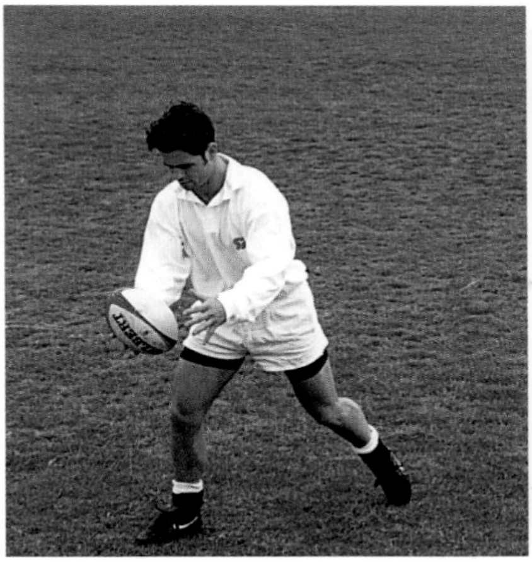

4

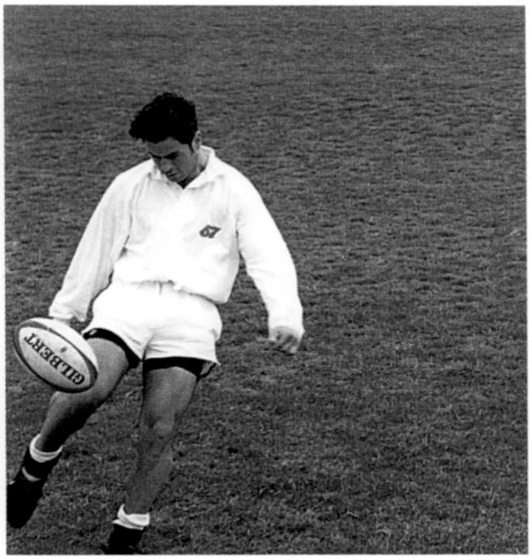

5

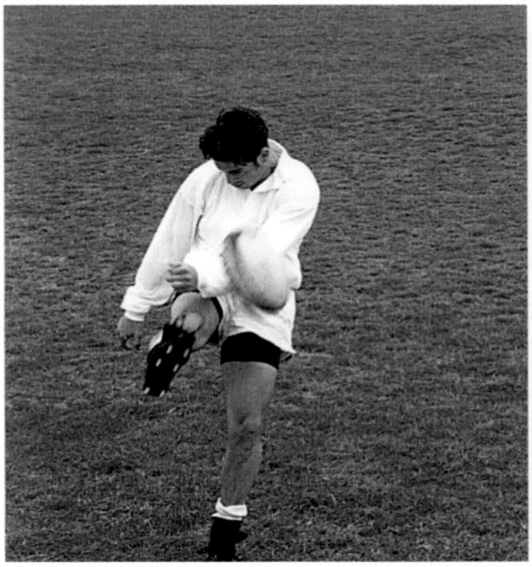

6

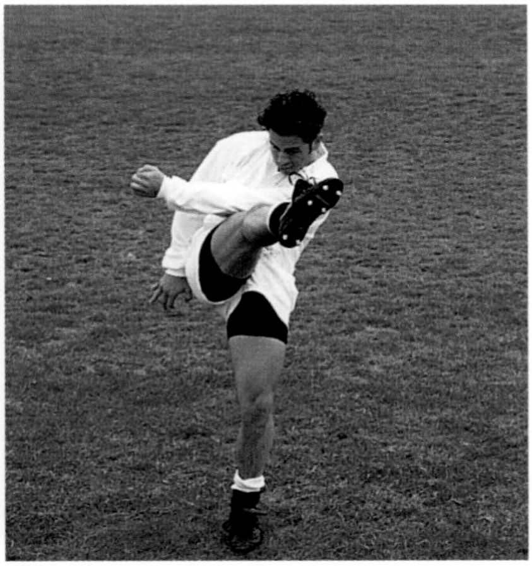

SCRUM-HALF PASSING

Instant
reaction

NEXT

The scrum-half pass is a specialised skill which requires a high degree of technical expertise and can only be perfected by a great deal of practice. There are four main situations for a scrum-half pass: from the base of a scrum or ruck at ground level; from a line-out or maul, where the ball is likely to be delivered around waist-level; the dive pass and the reverse pass, both of which can be necessary when the scrum-half has to react under pressure to a particular situation.

All four types of pass have a lot in common. They should be executed as fast and as accurately as possible. The key words are speed and accuracy. It is the job of the scrum-half to give as much time and space as possible to the fly-half and the threequarter line, so every split-second counts. But speed is no use without accuracy. If the pass is behind the fly-half, along the ground or over his head, any potential threequarter-line movement is dead and buried before it has begun. Similarly, if the pass is deadly accurate but the scrum-half takes all afternoon to wind up before unleashing the ball, the backs will have no room to do anything.

So the combination of speed and accuracy is what counts. The length of pass is also important, but definitely not as vital as the speed and accuracy. Nonetheless, there is no doubt that the spin pass is not only the best for speed and accuracy but also delivers the greatest distance. Having said that, whilst the pass should always be as fast and as accurate as possible, it should not always be thrown as far as possible. It should be far enough to give the fly-half and the backs the room they need to operate successfully but that will often be well within the maximum distance of the scrum-half's pass.

Kyran Bracken is capable of spin-passing from the base of the scrum 30 yards quickly and accurately, but a fly-half at international level like Rob Andrew would probably find somewhere between 15 and 20 yards the optimum distance. Of course, for young schoolchildren and mini-rugby players learning to play at half-back, it could well be that the maximum distance an eight-year-old scrum-half can spin-pass is 30 feet rather than 30 yards, and that his fly-half would be very happy with a pass of 15 or 20 feet.

Whatever the age of the scrum-half and whatever his aspirations or ambitions, the basic skills and ingredients of a good pass are exactly the same. The first priority is the correct position of the feet, the hands and the body.

Get those right and everything becomes easy; get them wrong and, inevitably, the speed and accuracy will suffer.

This is equally important for all the different types of scrum-half pass. England international scrum-half Kyran Bracken has arguably the fastest and most accurate service in the game today, but it should be stressed that this end-product is the result of thousands of hours of practice. Here he demonstrates all the major points.

THE SPIN PASS

The art of the spin pass is one of the most difficult skills to master initially and one of the best ways to learn it is to try passing off the ground with one hand only. I must stress that this should never be attempted in a match, but it is a very good way of learning to spin-pass. If the player is passing to his left, as Kyran demonstrates in this first sequence, the power of the pass is provided by the right hand.

1. To practise the spin pass the player should place his right hand on the ball exactly as Kyran is showing. I should emphasise that mini-rugby players will find it impossible to spin-pass a full-size rugby ball and they should use the size of ball appropriate to their age group. Note that the ball is just inside Kyran's right leg and his weight is mostly on his right leg. From this reasonably wide stance, with his hand on the top part of the ball and his fingers extended to a couple of inches below the middle of it, he begins the pass.

2. He propels the ball in a single flowing movement towards Paul Hull at fly-half. As he does so, most of his weight is transferred on to his left leg and at the same time he starts to rotate his hips, head, shoulders and eyes towards the fly-half. The right hand has turned through 90 degrees so that the palm of the hand is facing Kyran's face. It is that turning movement of the hand which imparts the spin.

3. The hand follows through with the scrum-half's body facing his fly-half and his eyes focused on his half-back partner.

1

2

3

One of the most important skills for every scrum-half is to learn to pass equally well in either direction. Every scrum-half ought to be able to pass quickly and accurately off either hand. Kyran demonstrates the one-handed pass with his left hand and all the same principles apply.

1. Left hand on the top half of the ball with fingers extended just past the middle of the ball, and the weight mostly on the left leg. The ball is just inside the left leg and eyes are on the ball.

2. The hand propels the ball in a single movement towards the fly-half. As Kyran does this, his weight is transferred on to the right leg and, at the same time, he rotates his hips, head, shoulders and eyes towards the fly-half. The left hand has turned through 90 degrees so the palm, which in the first picture in this sequence is facing fly-half Paul Hull. That turning action generates the spin.

3. This demonstrates the follow-through with the body and eyes facing the fly-half and the ball spinning in front of him ready for him to run on to it.

1

2

3

Both of these first two sequences are good methods of helping a scrum-half develop a spin pass. The next step is to do the same exercise using both hands as you would always do in a match. When passing to the left, the main power is provided by the right hand with the left hand helping to generate the spin effect underneath the ball. The left hand in this case also helps to ensure the accuracy of the pass.

1. As the ball emerges from a scrum or ruck, the scrum-half must immediately get his feet and body into the right position as his hands, simultaneously, go for the ball. Here, Kyran has the perfect wide base with the ball just inside the right foot. His eyes are fixed on the ball.

2. As his hands grasp the ball with his right hand, exactly as it was in picture 1 on page 91, he then turns his head towards his fly-half to focus on passing the ball a couple of yards in front of him so that the fly-half can run on to it. His weight at the beginning of the pass is mostly on the right leg.

3. The weight is now being transferred to the left leg as the ball is brought across the body in a single sweeping movement.

4. The scrum-half fixes his sights on the target area with his hands slightly crossing over as they each rotate through 90 degrees to create the spin pass.

5. A good follow-through with both hands pointing towards the fly-half.

1

2

3

4

5

Here the same sequence is shown with Paul Hull at fly-half to receive the ball.

1

2

Passing to the right demands the same disciplines and it is worth pointing out that part of the power comes from the legs as well as from the hands, arms, shoulders and body.

1. Feet in the correct position with the head over the ball, eyes fixed on the ball and hands ready to grasp the ball.

2. Hands on the ball and eyes still watching it.

3. As the ball is swept across the body in a single movement the head and shoulders begin to rotate towards the target area and most of the weight is transferred from the left leg to the right.

4. Both hands rotate as the ball is unleashed.

5. A good strong follow-through with the hands pointing at the target area.

3

4

5

Exactly the same as the previous
sequence, with Paul Hull at fly-half
to receive the ball.

It is very important with all these passes not only to have a wide base and for the scrum-half to bend right down in a squat position ready to uncoil and fire out a quick, accurate pass, but also that he makes sure he gives himself enough room to execute the pass. To ensure that he has a perfect view of his target area the foot nearest the fly-half must be far enough back to give him a clear view. If you draw a line through both feet it should point roughly at the fly-half.

This shows the correct angle, making it as easy as possible to deliver a fast, accurate pass.

1

2

3

PASSING FROM A LINE-OUT OR MAUL

All the same principles apply to scrum-half passing from a line-out or a maul, the only real difference being that the ball is usually delivered somewhere around waist-height and not at ground-level. Still the most important factors are having the feet in the right position and the hands ready to catch the ball and transfer it in one fast movement. If the feet are in the wrong position or the hands do not collect the ball in the right place, there will be a delay in delivering the pass. The first sign of a good scrum-half is a player who can instantly get his feet and hands in the correct position to deliver a swift, accurate pass the moment the ball is made available.

1. The scrum-half watches where the ball is thrown in the line-out and then quickly positions himself ready for the palm-down or the two-handed catch.

2. With feet adjusted rapidly to the flight of the ball from the jumper, Kyran watches the ball and prepares to catch it with his arms extended ready to whip the pass out in a single movement.

3. The moment he has his hands on the ball, his head, hips, body, shoulders and eyes begin to rotate towards the fly-half.

4. This shows a good follow-through at the target area, which will be a couple of yards in front of the fly-half so that he can run on to the ball.

The same pass, except that this time it is to the right and the fly-half is in vision.

1. Feet and hands are ready in the perfect position.

2. Eyes on the ball and both hands just outside the left-hand side of the body so there is no need for any backswing – the ball can be delivered in one single movement immediately.

3. Hands on the ball, and you can see that a straight line drawn from Kyran's left foot to his right foot and then extended for 20 yards would be aiming right at his target area. It is worth noting that he has made a slight adjustment with the placing of his right foot between pictures 1 and 3 to get his angle correct.

4. Head, body, hips, shoulders and eyes rotate towards the target area.

5. A good follow-through with the ball in front of the fly-half ready for him to run on to it.

6. Paul Hull takes the ball and would now be ready to unleash his backs.

1

2

3

4

5

6

1
2

THE DIVE PASS

There are occasions in most matches when, for whatever reason, the ball is not presented perfectly to the scrum-half by the forwards. In tight situations or when the scrum-half is under intense pressure from the opposition, he may find it to his advantage to make a dive pass. This can happen when his own scrum is being pushed backwards, or the ball pops out at the wrong angle, or the line-out jumpers palm the ball back well away from him; whenever he has to scamper a few steps to get to the ball a dive pass might be the best option. Similarly, on a wet day or on a muddy pitch, the dive pass protects both the ball and the scrum-half.

1. The scrum-half approaches the loose ball in a crouching position, hands outstretched and eyes on the ball.

2. On reaching it, both hands grasp the ball and one foot is positioned just behind the ball ready to provide the drive and momentum behind the pass. Here Kyran Bracken places his right leg just behind the ball so in this instance this one will be the driving leg. Either leg is equally effective, but remember it will take most of the weight as the player launches himself into the pass. The dive pass is always made off one leg.

3. Now Kyran turns his head upwards to focus his eyes on his target and launches the ball and himself towards his fly-half, Paul Hull.

4. With the scrum-half in mid-flight, the ball is spinning to the fly-half. Once again, the wrists, by rotating, impart the spin to the ball.

5. The hands lead the body as they drive through the ball. The whole body weight has been propelled forwards and upwards which helps to give good elevation to the ball.

6. Kyran lands a couple of metres from his take-off point. Note that his eyes are still fixed on the receiver and that if you drew a straight line from his feet to his head it would be pointing straight at the fly-half.

Having completed the pass, the scrum-half should bounce back on to his feet and follow the ball in support.

THE REVERSE PASS

There will be occasions when the ball is in the wrong place for an orthodox pass and time is of the essence. The reverse pass is the hardest pass of all to master, but it is also the most spectacular if done well. Once again, the position of the feet and body are important and the scrum-half needs to be well balanced because in the reverse pass, the player's body momentum is going in the opposite direction to the receiver.

For this special pass, the shoulders and arms play a more significant role in providing the real power rather than the legs and the hips.

The player should be almost stationary when making the pass because balance is important. More often than not, the reverse pass comes into play because something has gone wrong and the scrum-half is not only under great pressure but also has to whip out a quick pass whilst he is facing in the wrong direction.

1. Initially the weight has to be on one foot. Here Kyran approaches the loose ball preparing to pass off his right leg, so that is the leg about to take his weight.

2. With his weight on his right leg, he places his hands on the ball and begins to transfer some of his weight on to his left leg.

3. With the weight now evenly distributed between both legs, he turns his eyes towards the receiver and prepares to pass.

4. Still focusing his eyes on his fly-half, he propels the ball towards him.

5. The pass is given from a fairly wide base and a strong follow-through is essential. Again, by slightly rotating the hands, it is possible to obtain the spinning action from a reverse pass.

This is not an easy pass and a young scrum-half must be prepared to put in many hours of practice to become skilled at it.

1

2

3

4

5

The final sequence in this section shows the reverse pass from a line-out, where the ball appears around waist-height but not in the right place for a normal spin pass. Instead, it is going to be quicker to undertake a reverse pass and the sequence looks very similar to the reverse pass off the ground.

TACKLING

Total commitment

NEXT

When it comes to choosing their favourite skills not many young players would put tackling near the top of the list but if you learn the correct technique from the start you will soon overcome any reservations and grow to appreciate how important good tackling is to every team. Any side made up of 15 fiercely competitive tacklers will be very hard to beat and the sooner young players learn to tackle the better.

At the outset it is a question of building up confidence and it is wrong to expect too much too soon. For the first few training sessions it is a good idea to have the defender on his knees on the ground with the attacker approaching at a slow walking pace.

In this way every player can learn all the proper techniques and discover that not only is it a relatively straightforward skill, but you do not get hurt when you put in a good tackle. Every player should practise tackling from the right using his right shoulder and from the left using his left shoulder.

Gradually, the exercise can be speeded up over several sessions until the attacker is running quite fast and the tackler is no longer on his knees but actually driving into the tackle. An equally good way of practising tackling initially is to use tackling bags. You might well be happier to throw yourself wholeheartedly at a tackling bag, safe in the knowledge that you won't be injured by a stray boot or knee or elbow.

The vital factor is to build up confidence gradually and not to rush. You could start with a tackling bag and go on to practise all the different types of tackle at walking pace, then trotting, then running at half-pace, followed by threequarter pace and finally flat out. And remember, a sound technique will inspire confidence.

It is advisable to start with the side-on tackle, from both the left and right, before advancing to the tackle from behind, the head-on tackle and the smother tackle.

I

THE SIDE-ON TACKLE

From the right

1. I line up my tackle on Rob Andrew and I know I will be using my right shoulder to make the tackle.

2. I close in and focus on the target area, which is just below waist-level. I prepare to drive into the tackle off one leg and not two. I will be using my right shoulder so I drive off my right leg.

3. As I drive into the tackle, using my full body weight, I hit the attacker with my right shoulder just below his hips and make sure I slip my head behind him and not in any circumstances in front of him. At the same time I wrap my arms firmly round his legs.

4. The combined impetus of my shoulder hitting him, the force of my full weight driving into the tackle and my arms being tightly wrapped round his legs makes it inevitable that he will topple over.

5. Assuming I have gone into the tackle aggressively, the likelihood is that I will end up on top of the tackled player.

2

3

4

5

From the left

This shows the same sequence using the left shoulder as I tackle side-on from the left.

I

THE TACKLE FROM BEHIND

The same principles apply to the tackle from behind as to the side-on tackle. The tackler drives into the tackle off one leg, hits the attacker with one shoulder between his knees and his hips, slips his head to one side and wraps his arms in a firm grip round his opponent's legs.

1. I line up Rob Andrew and decide which side to tackle him.

2. I choose to use my right shoulder, so that I accelerate into the tackle, hitting him with my shoulder just below the hips and making sure my head is to the left of his left leg. At the same time I wrap my arms round his legs to stop him in his tracks.

3. With the momentum built up as I accelerated into the tackle, the force of my full weight behind it and by hanging on to his legs, he is bound to crash to the ground.

4. As I pull him down I should finish up on top of the tackled player.

2

3

4

1

2

THE HEAD-ON TACKLE

This is one of the more difficult tackles to make and it can be done in two different ways. If the tackler is far lighter than the attacker then he would be well advised to allow the much bigger man to fall over him in the tackle. If, on the other hand, the tackler is the bigger, heavier player he can try to knock the ball-carrier backwards and finish on top of him. Here, with the help of Rob Andrew, I demonstrate both methods.

1. Assuming that either Rob Andrew is bigger than me or that he has got up a full head of steam and I am fairly static in this particular situation, I decide that discretion is the better part of valour and I will not try to knock him backwards. I line him up on my left shoulder and prepare to make the tackle.

2. I hit him with my left shoulder just below his hips, carefully placing my head outside his left leg. On this occasion the attacker is running faster than me so I know I am not going to be able to knock him backwards.

3   **4**

3. I wrap my arms round his legs and his greater speed and momentum mean that he goes over me in the tackle.

4. I have clung tightly to his legs throughout this operation so he has no alternative but to crash to the ground.

The theory about the head-on tackle is quite simple. If two players of similar size are travelling at the same speed, the attacker will probably go up in the air and land to the side of the tackler. If the attacker is travelling much faster than the defender, he will probably go over his shoulder, as has happened in the above sequence.

If the defender can accelerate into the tackle and be travelling faster than the ball-carrier, then he can knock him backwards as we see in this next sequence.

1. I prepare to accelerate towards the attacker and drive into the tackle off one leg with the intention of hitting him back quite forcibly.

2. I hit him hard with my right shoulder just below the hips and, having accelerated into the tackle and having the impetus of my full weight driving through, I hold the initiative.

3. With the force of my tackle and with my arms clasped firmly around his legs, the ball-carrier is knocked backwards.

4. As I was calling all the shots in this tackle, I end up on top.

1

2

3

4

1

2

THE SMOTHER TACKLE

This is a special tackle which aims not only to stop the ball-carrier making any further ground but also to prevent him from passing to any of his supporting team-mates.

It is the one tackle where the target is not below the hips but well above the waist, as the tackler is trying to engulf his opponent's arms so that he can't deliver any sort of pass and, in consequence, to abruptly halt his team's attacking momentum.

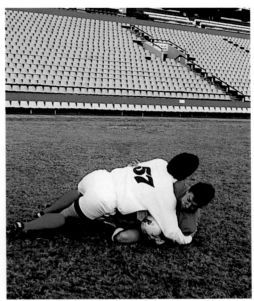

3   **4**

1. I approach the ball-carrier in a more upright stance than usual as I will be tackling above waist-level.

2. I still accelerate into the tackle and hit the attacker hard with my right shoulder around his shoulders whilst at the same instant I try to wrap my arms right round his upper body so that the ball is trapped and so are his arms.

3. Still driving forwards and downwards, and making sure that the ball is smothered somewhere between us, we will both hit the deck.

4. As I drove into the tackle more forcibly and with the greater impetus, I finish on top on the ground.

Although it is not a skill beginners particularly relish, tackling is a very important part of the game and everyone has to learn to do it properly. As players get older they could well find they get just as much pleasure and satisfaction from a great try-saving tackle as from scoring a great try.

The truth is that the more basic skills a player has, the more enjoyment he will derive from rugby.

You get out of the game what you put in to it. It is definitely worth making that supreme effort to master all rugby's basic skills.

The earlier you do it the better and you can look forward to many years of fun and enjoyment.

And remember, the more you practise the better you become.